# Love's Undivided Light

Beyond This World: A Journey to the
Heart of Being

Maureen Lynch Yarbrough,
O.M.C.

BookLeaf Publishing

India | USA | UK

Made with ❤ on the BookLeaf Publishing Platform
www.bookleafpub.in
www.bookleafpub.com

# Dedication

For Brody, Brianna, and Paige (DIL), my children, and Moriah, Marcus, and Melea, my grandchildren (at the time of publishing!) - you hold all my heart.

May these poems whisper truths of love and oneness, inspiring you to discover the light within yourselves.

And to the future branches of our family tree, may you too find your way to the heart of Being.

I love you all more than words can express. I pray that you feel it. Please remember how precious and amazing you are. Pause with the Holy Spirit and you can't go wrong.

You are the light of this world. Keep shining!

Lastly, to my "special" love, Freddie. You light up my every day. Thank you for walking beside me on this journey of love & forgiveness. Thank you for allowing me to feel your beautiful heart, and soul, and for demonstrating your love on a daily basis. You are a constant reminder of the truth that lies within me. Your presence is an amazing gift. I am eternally grateful. Our love stands as a testament to the beauty in this world, to be sure.


And to all of my siblings and parents - by blood or marriage. I love you all dearly, and each of you reside in my heart.

# Acknowledgement

"A Course in Miracles," scribed by Helen Schucman and Bill Thetford, is a work of profound spiritual insight. I gratefully acknowledge their role in bringing this inspired teaching to the world.

I would also like to acknowledge all the pain and training in forgiveness I have transversed, and will continue to navigate...each are a lesson that results in my awakening to Truth.

# Preface

My hope is that these poems will resonate with you, evoking a sense of recognition and reminding you of the beauty and truth that reside within each of us. May they offer a moment of reflection, a whisper of hope, and a connection to the oneness that unites us all.

I would like to thank all of the A Course in Miracles teachers and students out there (as we are both, no?). Each of you have assisted in my journey and I am so very grateful.

# Beyond the Rift

No control, though I believe I do.
My hands grasp at smoke, a phantom clue.

I forget so often...absolutely.
Like dreams that fade with morning clarity.
But...
Not the Truth!

Truth is the stillness in a hurricane's eye,
A single star in the vast night sky.

It is not when I am frantic, bewildered,
A tangled head, feeling abused,
Not a victim of illness, self-accused!

I want all to be perfect, a flawless art,
People to act as I wish, all with heart.

That's pure insanity...a house built on sand,
And will only cause a rift, a divided land.

Separation of any kind, a chasm deep,
Does not unite, but sows seeds we weep.

It's in the Oneness, the interwoven chain,
That I find the Divine, where peace will reign.

Labels used are a sharpened stone,
And discrimination, a heart turned to bone,
Causing a divide, a world unknown.

But in the stillness, a whisper I find,
The truth unveiled, for heart and mind,
In every moment, Oneness entwined.

Exhale the fear, inhale the Love.
And all is right with this Divine Hug!

# The Ego's Fallacy

This body, a whisper, a passing dream,
Cannot hold the vastness of what you seem.
You are not bone, nor flesh's embrace,
But a boundless Spirit, in time and space.

This form, the me-Ego's earthly play,
A logic's dance in the light of day.
But it cannot define the soul's deep core,
The truth of your being, forevermore.

The ego boasts, "I am the one! My will be
done,
my victories won!"
Separate, unique, it seeks its throne,
A hollow echo, utterly alone.

But this pursuit leads to endless strife,
Fear's dark shadow, a wasted life.
The Self you yearn for, pure and bright,
Shines within, a guiding light.

Rest in the beauty of Who you are,
And joy will bloom like a distant star.

Peace will descend, doubts take flight,
In this true Self, Divine and bright.

Listening closely to this inner call,
You'll walk with grace, and stand up tall.
No need to hurry, no need to fear,
In service to Self, your path is always, always
clear.

# As It Is

The world I see is a projection of my own
mind.
I yearn for my perception to let go...unwind,

Those beliefs, fears, and judgments I hold
onto dearly,
I yearn to experience the freedom of all labels
and see clearly.

I believe I am separate from God and from all
others.
This separation is the root of all of my inner
suffering and druthers.

It is in healing the mind, that I change my
experience of this world.
Kindness, compassion, and love are
expressions of my true nature,
which is oneness with God—-complete.
Unfurled.

The means by which I heal the illusion of
separation.
 Even if the world is an illusion, my
experience of it is very real,
and my actions have real consequences in this
living situation.

Acts of kindness are not just about helping
others;
they are about healing my own mind.
By extending love, I recognize my own
inherent lovableness
—ah, what a find!

The world is a classroom where I learn to
forgive
and awaken to my true nature.
Kindness is a fundamental lesson in this
laboratory.
Ahhh...rapture!

Detachment from the ego's drama is
imperative
but indifference to the suffering of others
—-not a worthy narrative.

True detachment means releasing judgment
and fear,
allowing us to respond with love and
compassion steering our being.

To use the "unreality" of the world as an
excuse to be unkind,
Leaves one deeply entrenched in ego, a
troubled state of mind.

Living a life of love and forgiveness, is all I
truly desire,
To feel the Holy Spirits guidance, setting my
soul afire.

Kindness is the way I demonstrate that we are
all One,
Love's acts multiply, until our journey is done.

# My Son

My son, eyes of green.
A mind so bright, a soul so keen.
My son, a mirror, reflecting what I knew,
A shadow cast by anger, a path we both
walked through.

The echoes of my struggles, a lesson learned
too late,
When separation's sorrow sealed a twist of
fate.
At ten years old, a parting, a father's guiding
hand,
A consequence of choices, I struggled to
withstand.

The weight of guilt, a burden, a constant,
heavy toll,
A mother's heart in pieces, losing all control.
Yet, in the depths of sorrow, a seed of hope
took root,
A yearning for redemption, to bear life's
bitter fruit.

Though paths diverged, and miles intervened,
The bond of mother and son, forever
convened.
For love will always transcend the trials we
endure,
And in each passing moment, we find a
chance to make pure.

To learn from past mistakes, to rise above the
pain,
And build a bridge of healing, where love can
bloom again.
I see your strength, your resilience, your
grace,
A spirit shining brightly, in time and in space.

I celebrate the man you've come to be,
Your heart of gold, for all the world to see.
For love is not defined by moments lost,
But by the hope and healing, no matter the
cost.

My love for you, a constant, guiding star,
A bond that shines forever, no matter where
you are.

Through every trial's challenge, through joy's triumphant flight,
My love, a constant anchor, will guide you through the night.
For a mother's love, a lifeline, unwavering and deep,
A guiding star to lead you, a lightness you can keep.

So let the past dissolve, like whispers in the wind,
Know my love surrounds you, a peace you'll always find.
For nothing you can do, and nothing you can say,
Can ever break the bond of my love for you, each and every day.

# My Daughter

A tiny cry, a jaundiced hue,
My baby girl, with eyes of blue.
They took you then, a cruel divide,
And left me empty, deep inside.

Those loving eyes, a trusting gaze,
Reflected back my hazy days.
You are my sunshine, pure and bright,
My sweet redemption, in the night.

But shadows crept, and darkness grew,
A tangled web, I pulled you through.
The discipline I should have shown,
Was lost, and seeds of chaos were sown.

My fractured mind, a broken plea,
Led me astray, away from thee.
To chase a ghost, a fleeting high,
And leave you weeping, wondering why.

The weight of failure, hard to bear,
A mother's guilt, beyond repair.

Through every trial and triumph, through
every joy and pain,
My love will be your anchor, in sunshine and
in rain.

For a mother's love, a beacon, shining ever
bright,
A guiding star to lead you, through darkness
into light.

So let the past dissolve, like mist before the
dawn,
And know my love surrounds you, forever
and anon.

For nothing you can do, and nothing you can
say,
Can ever break the bond that love has forged
the day you were born.

I love you.

# A Mother's Failure

The years unfold, a tapestry of gray,
Where threads of "what ifs" forever sway.
A mother's heart, a heavy, burdened stone,
Reflects the seeds of choices poorly sown.
Too young, too lost, a storm within her
breast,
She sought solace, found a restless quest.
The rules unlearned, the boundaries blurred
and faint,
A gentle hand, replaced by weak restraint.
She sees the echoes in her children's eyes,
The mirrored flaws, the whispered, sad
goodbyes.
The lessons missed, the guidance left undone,
A mother's failure, beneath a setting sun.
The stress, a shadow, clinging to her soul,
A whispered mantra, taking its dark toll. "If
only," the words that haunt her dreams,
A river flowing, with regretful streams.
The fractured home, a guilt she can't erase,
The broken vows, the tears upon her face. The
constant moves, a restless, shifting ground,
Where roots could never firmly be found.

The weight of divorce, a heavy, unseen chain,
A constant failure, a relentless pain.
She shattered their world, or so it seemed,
And chased a phantom, a half-forgotten
dream.
No harsh intent, no malice in her core,
Just youthful blindness, knocking at the door.
A lack of wisdom, in a hurried race,
To find her footing, in life's chaotic space.
She yearns to mend, to stitch the tattered
seams,
To offer solace, and to heal their dreams.
But time, a thief, has stolen precious days,
And left her standing, in remorseful haze.

# A New Beginning

The veil, a silk so finely spun,
Begins to shift, the day is done.
A hush descends, a whispered plea,
The rattle hours, wild and often scary.
The body, once a vibrant bloom,
Now softens, yielding to the tomb.
A gentle fading, slow and profound,
A quiet beauty, secret bound.
The skin, a parchment, cool and pale,
Where life's bright story begins to fail.
But in that stillness, grace resides,
A peaceful journey, where love abides.
The soul, a bird, with wings unfurled,
Prepares to part this earthly world.
No fear, no darkness, just release,
A silent flight, a tranquil peace.
At bedside's edge, the shadows gleam,
Visions arise, a waking dream.
Faces beloved, long since flown,
Return to guide, and claim their own.
A whispered welcome, soft and low,
As loved ones gather, to and fro.

They wait to lead, with gentle hand,
To realms unseen, a promised land.
The leaving light, a golden thread,
Unravels softly, overhead.
No final gasp, no anguished cry,
Just gentle passing, by and by.
For death's embrace, a tender art,
A closing chapter, a fresh start.
A transformation, pure and bright,
A soul's ascension, into light.

# My Three M's, My Heart's Delight

Three shining stars, a wondrous sight,
My three M's, my pure delight!

A tapestry of love is spun,
My precious treasures, every one.

Moriah, with an artist's soul,
Where colors dance and stories roll.
A world of beauty, you create,
A masterpiece, sealed by fate.

Marcus, with a basketball's grace,
A soaring leap, a winning chase.
With every shot, a heart takes flight,
A champion's spirit, shining bright.

And Melea, so sweet and cute.
With eyes that shine with love and
deviousness, to boot!
A gentle touch, a happy sound,
Where boundless joy is always found.

You love your siblings, hand in hand,
A precious bond, a grand stand!

Together you grow, a family's art,
Forever held within my heart.
My darlings, know, beyond all measure,
My love for you, a timeless treasure.

More than words can ever say,
You brighten every single day.
So let your spirits ever soar,
And know my love, forevermore.

My three M's, my pride, my glee!
Magical beings, eternally!

# Respect, A Gift to Self

A seed of kindness, buried deep,
A gentle promise - one must keep.

Respect, a word, a simple grace,
Reflected in this world of time and space.

For every soul, a hidden fire,
A worth that burns, a fierce desire.

To be acknowledged, seen, and heard,
A silent, yet resounding word.

Though paths may differ, views collide,
And storms of anger churn inside,

The core remains, a fragile thing,
A human heart that longs to sing.

No matter stature, age, or creed,
No matter triumph, or the need,

To lift another, not to break,
A sacred, silent vow to make.

For in the giving, we receive,
A woven tapestry, believe.

Respect, a mirror, bright and clear,
Reflecting what we hold so dear.

A whispered "please," a patient ear,
A hand that reaches through the fear.

A simple nod, a gentle gaze,
Respect, through all our passing days.

Let empathy be our guiding light,
To chase away the darkest night.

And understand, with open eyes,
Respect, a gift that never dies.

# Rattle No More

The rattle comes, a breathy sigh,
A sound that makes the living cry.

It scrapes and whispers, rough and low,
A fear that loved ones often know.

But believe this truth, and hold it near,
No pain resides, no cause for fear.

The body shifts, its work near done,
The lungs, they falter, one by one.

The fluids gather, soft and deep,
A gentle slumber, while they sleep.

The throat, it echoes, faint and frail,
A final, earthly, whispered tale.

It's not a struggle, not a fight,
But nature's rhythm, in fading light.

The soul prepares to take its flight,
Beyond the reach of all you might...

Envision.

So when the rattle fills the air,
Release your sorrow, quell all despair.

It's not a sign of pain or dread,
But peaceful passage, gently led.

Imagine waves upon the shore,
Receding softly, evermore.

The body rests, the spirit free,
A sweet and deep tranquility.

Let gentle hands and loving eyes,
Bring comfort as the moment flies.

And know that in that final sound,
A peaceful leaving will be found.

# Reflection

A shadow falls, a whispered sting,
A judgment cast, a wounded thing.

The words, like stones, begin to weigh,
And darkness threatens to hold you away...

But in the stillness, soft and deep,
A gentle truth begins to creep.

Not in the fault, the spoken blame,
But in the heart, a flickering flame.

For what is seen, a mirrored glass,
Reflects the fears that swiftly pass.

The critic's voice, a troubled plea,
A longing for tranquility.

Forgive the tongue, the hasty word,
A soul in darkness, barely heard.

Release the weight, the heavy chain,
And let compassion ease the pain.

The peace within, a steady light,
Will banish shadows of the night.

No outer storm can truly bind,
The quiet strength within the mind.

# My Special Love

Thirteen years, a thread unseen, a quiet,
distant rhyme,
Acquaintances we lingered, unaware of what
we would find.

Then, "forgiveness" whispered, a word that
drew you near,
A reason to connect, dispelling every fear.

Your heart, by my words on Facebook, a
gentle pull confessed,
A yearning to explore, to set your soul at rest.

Forgiveness, our excuse, a bridge we dared to
cross,
A coffee date's soft promise, of joining to
discuss.

Memorial Day's solemn call, a Harley's
gleaming might,
A journey to my parent's gravesides, bathed in
the sun's shining light.

Your glistening arms, a strength, a tender,
guiding sway,
Gripping the bars on the motorcycle, on that
sacred, hallowed day.

Cracker Barrel's comfort, and Pam, our five
star delight.
This feeling that consumed me stirred me
with trepidation and fright.

A sense of deep connection, a knowing,
ancient grace,
Though years between us lingered, in this
familiar space.

Eighteen years a whisper, a shadow in the air,
But souls entwined forever, beyond all earthly
care.

Time held no power over this love that burns
so bright,
Our spirits recognized each other - souls
colliding in the night.

A hesitant first goodbye, a fear within your
gaze,
A kiss unspoken, lost in twilight's hazy maze.

Past hurts and despairs, barriers we defied,
For destiny's sweet promise, would keep us
side by side.

For we were meant to be, two halves that
found their peace,
A love that blossomed freely, a soul's eternal
lease.

My true love, my soul mate, a gift beyond
compare,
Your presence is my solace, a love beyond all
care.

I love you, Freddie.

# Bold & Beautiful Heart

In chaos swirling, a world gone slightly mad,
Where shadows lengthen, and hearts grow
cold and sad,

Remember Who you are, a light within the
fray,
A beacon of compassion, to guide and grace
the day.

The storm may rage around, and voices rise in
fear,
But anchor deep your soul, let Truth be ever
near.

Stand firm in integrity, a mountain strong
and tall,
Let kindness be your compass, answering
every call.

Inclusion's gentle whisper, a bridge across the
divide,
Where every heart is welcome, with nothing
left to hide.

Let Love be your foundation, a shelter from
the storm,
A warmth that mends the shattered, and
keeps the spirit warm.

When anger seeks to claim you, and
bitterness takes hold,
Resist the urge to react, let wisdom make you
bold.

Respond with gentle spirit, with patience and
with grace,
And find the strength to offer, a loving, calm
embrace.

Though darkness may surround you, and
doubt may cloud your sight,
Keep faith alive within you, and let your
spirit Light!

For on this globe, where shadows dance and
gleam,
Your heart, a steady flame, a hopeful, vibrant
dream.

Remember Who you are, a soul of gentle
might,
A star that shines so brightly, in the darkest,
deepest night.

Allow your love and kindness, a healing balm
impart,
A testament to courage, within a bold and
beautiful heart.

# Abandonment's Echo

A whispered fear, a story etched in pain,
Abandonment's echo, a life-long, driving rain.
No steady hand, no constant, gentle guide,
A childhood's fractured pieces, where sorrows
did reside.

A mother's fleeting shadow, a vacant, empty
space,
Five children left alone, in time's relentless
chase.
A baby's hungry cry, a sister's desperate deed,
Mustard sandwiches stolen, a desperate,
meager feed.

A father's bold escape, a Navy's broken vow,
To rescue fragile lives, and shield them
somehow.
From Virginia's troubled shores, to New
York's distant sway,
With an Aunt's acceptance of these young
lives, where hope began to play.

Then Maine's cold whispers, another Aunt's domain,
A shifting landscape, where roots could not remain.
At seven, California's promise, a father's longed-for sight,
A hero's welcome, bathed in golden light.

But joy turned bitter, a mother's cruel decree,
A brother's shattered heart, a pain for me to see.
My Daddy's girl's devotion, a sacrifice so deep,
To shield a brother's sorrow, secrets mom would keep.

At ten a new stepmom's presence, a journey's winding trail,
An RV's rolling thunder, across the weathered vale.
From LA's bustling streets, to Oregon's green embrace,
Then Long Island's restless spirit, a nomadic, hurried pace.

From town to town, a life in constant flight,
Change became a comfort in endless day and
night.

Following a broken path, my mother's
shadowed trace,
Alcohol's dark comfort, and fleeting, human
grace.
Men, like fleeting shadows, a desperate,
hollow plea, A fear of solitude, a longing to
be free.
Yet, from the depths of chaos, a resilient spirit
soared,
A life reclaimed, no more alcohol to be
poured.
Though scars remain, a testament to strife,
Gratitude's bright beacon now illuminates my
daily life.
From shattered fragments, a strength I
bravely found,
A thriving soul reborn, on hallowed, solid
ground.

# More Than This Body

Shed the skin, the form, the earthly guise,
For you are more than what within the mirror
lies.

A spirit unbound, a soul forever free,
One with the energy of Love's vast sea.

Not flesh and bone, but starlight's gentle
gleam,
A cosmic dance, a universal dream.

Your world, a canvas, painted by beliefs,
A tapestry woven, bringing joy or grief.

At your heart's core, innocence resides,
Like newborn babes, where pure potential
hides.

No need for pardon, no sins to confess,
For all you witness, your own mind's address.

Perception's lens, a filter, time-worn and old,
Projecting shadows, stories yet untold.

The past's dark echoes, the future's anxious
plea,
Distort the present, and steal your liberty.

Only this moment, where stillness finds its
grace,
Let go of longing, find your sacred space.

Expectations crumble, like castles built on
sand,
As freedom's whisper guides your gentle hand.

Embrace the joy, the lightness of your soul,
Where love's pure current makes your spirit
whole.

No judgment cast, no condemnation's sting,
Only compassion, on love's ethereal wing.

For in this unity, where hearts as one convene,
The truth unfolds, a love forever keen.

# My Why

My Why, a sunrise bursting, brilliant and
bold,
In every grandchild's giggle, tales yet untold.
My children's laughter echoes, a melody so
sweet,
My beloved's strong presence makes life
complete.

The furry chorus sings, a love that knows no
bounds,
Six four-paws that dance around me, on
hallowed, joyful grounds.

My Why, a breaking free, from shadows that
confine,
A soul released from burdens, a peaceful,
vibrant mind.

It's the wild exhilaration, on paths where
truth is found,
A heart that leaps with purpose, on
consecrated ground.

My Why, a hand extended, in service to the whole,
A vessel for compassion, to heal a weary soul.

It's the light that shines within me, a beacon in the night,
A living testament to freedom, and spirit's soaring flight.

My Why, to dance in joy, beneath the open sky,
To trace the running trails of wonder, where dreams and spirits fly.

It's walking hand-in-hand, through life's unfolding stage,
From wedding bells to whispers, on grief's sorrowful page.

To guide the soul's awakening, to truth's revealing grace,
And offer gentle comfort, in every sacred space.

To be the voice of solace, when shadows
gather near,
To banish lonely echoes, and quell the rising
fear.

My Why, a vibrant current, flowing wild and
free,
The truest, purest essence, of all that I can Be.

It's love that knows no limits, no boundaries
to define,
A heart that beats in rhythm, with a Love
that's truly Thine.

My Why, a radiant fire, burning ever bright,
A testament to all with Love's eternal light.

# My Purpose

My Purpose: to ignite a spark, a dawn within
each soul,
In grandchildren's bright eyes, where future
stories roll.
To weave my children's laughter, a tapestry of
grace,
And stand beside my partner, in life's
unwavering space.

To amplify the love songs, the furry hearts
impart,
Six four-paws that leave their prints, upon my
grateful heart.

My Purpose: to dismantle walls, where
shadows held me bound,
And plant the seeds of freedom, on hallowed,
fertile ground.

To blaze a trail of Truth, where hidden
pathways lead,
And cultivate the courage, to plant a noble
seed.

My Purpose: to extend my hands, a bridge to
those in need,
To be a living vessel, where compassion takes
the lead.
To kindle inner lanterns, when darkness fills
the air,
And fan the flames of hope, beyond all
earthly care.

My Purpose: to dance in joy, beneath the sun's
warm gaze,
And trace the maps of wonder, through life's
enchanting maze.

To walk beside the weary, through life's
unfolding play,
From wedding vows to whispers, that chase
the grief away.
To spark the soul's awakening, and guide
them to their core,
And offer gentle comfort, when hearts are
bruised and sore.

To be a voice of healing, when loneliness
descends,
And banish fear's dark echoes, that silently
transcend.

My Purpose: to unleash the hidden strength,
that flows eternally,
The truest, purest essence, of all we are meant
to Be.

To love without restraint, a force that knows
no end,
A heart that beats in rhythm, with a love that
will transcend.

My Purpose: to be a flame, that burns with
vibrant might,
A testament to living, in Love's transforming
light.

# Ahh....Running

At forty-eight, a journey unforeseen,
A runner's heart, where it had never been.
The treadmill's hum, 13.1 miles, a Covid-era
start,
Virtual friends surrounding me, mending a
broken heart.

A love-hate dance, a struggle and a grace,
Some runs are a battle, testing time and
space.

"I never regret a run," a mantra strong and
true,
A whispered promise, pushing bravely
through.

From 5Ks' swiftness, to trails' untamed
delight,
Where nature's beauty shines both day and
night.

A marathon's first trial, a grueling, painful
fight,
Post-illness shadows, dimming inner light.
Yet, Coach Amy's wisdom, a steady, guiding
hand,
"Don't quit," she urged, on this demanding
land.
The final miles walked, a lesson dearly
learned,
A spirit tested, a new resolve discerned.

Redemption's marathon, with Holly by my
side,
A glorious victory, where dreams and spirits
ride.

New York's grand marathon, a city girl's
embrace,
A homecoming triumph, in that familiar
space.

Twelve hours stretched, a challenge to defy,
Forty-six miles conquered, beneath a watchful
sky.

Then fifty miles claimed, in 2024's bold stride,
A testament to will, where inner forces abide.

Post-Covid's lingering trials, thyroid's subtle
sting,
But still, the hundred-mile dream, takes flight
on hopeful wing.

Mind over matter, a truth that burns so
bright,
A runner's transformation, bathed in sacred
light.

No athlete's past, no legacy to claim,
Just passion's fire, a burning, vibrant flame.

For Sean, my brother, taken far too soon,
His spirit runs beside me, beneath the sun
and moon.
His athletic prowess, a legacy I embrace,
His memory a strength, in my every running
pace.

He carries me onward, a love that knows no
end,
My brother, my companion, my ever-present
friend.

# Go Forth!

The landscape of fear, a mist-shrouded way,
Where whispers of "cannot" attempt to lead
astray.
But step by hesitant step, a journey you
embrace,
To navigate the shadows, and find your sacred
space.

Each trembling breath, a victory hard-won,
A battle fought with courage, beneath the
rising sun.
For in the heart of fear, a hidden strength
resides,
A power waiting to awaken, where true
potential lies.

Once fear is faced and conquered, its grip
begins to cease,
A surge of liberation, a soul released in peace.
No longer held by limits, the mind's illusions
spun,
But rising on the wings of what you have
Be-come.

Imposter syndrome's echoes, a phantom's
hollow call,
A fabricated doubt, that seeks to make you
fall.
Let others shine their brilliance, their unique
path to trace,
Your voice, your truth, your purpose, will find
its rightful place.

For every soul is gifted, with a message to
convey,
To touch the lives of others, and light their
darkened way.
Embrace your strength, your journey, your
inner radiant fire,
And stand in your own power, lifting spirits
higher.

Don't let the shadows dim the truth that
burns so bright,
Remember who you are, a beacon of pure
light.
One with the divine essence, a spirit strong
and bold,
A child of boundless grace, a story to unfold.

So walk through fear's dark valley, with
courage as your guide,
And follow your heart's compass, where
destiny resides.
Keep your focus forward where the realm of
wonders waits,
Where conquering fear unlocks, your soul's
triumphant gates.

# Seeds of Love

Within the heart's deep chamber,
where faith's soft whispers dwell,
A truth unfolds, a story that each soul knows
well.
We are One with God, a love that knows no
end,
A radiant, timeless essence, a faithful, trusted
friend.

The world's illusion shatters, when Love
becomes our guide,
For fear's dark, grasping tendrils, can no
longer then abide.
Yet egos rise like shadows, with judgments
sharp and cold,
Comparing, labeling, criticizing - stories to
be told.

But these are fleeting echoes, not the spirit's
true domain,
We must recall our Oneness, and break the
ego's chain.

For in remembering Who we are, a light
begins to gleam,
And others find their pathway, within that
sacred dream.

Though terror may surround us, and sorrow
fill the air,
We choose to be compassion, a love beyond
compare.
To lend a helping hand, with kindness in our
gaze,
But not to be consumed, by fear's bewildering
maze.

Acceptance is our anchor, in life's tumultuous
sea,
Let go of what is fleeting, and find serenity.
For what we cannot alter, let gently drift
away,
And trust in God's great wisdom, to guide us
through each day.

Remember, thoughts are seeds, that blossom
in the mind,
Love's gentle whispers nurture, while fear
leaves scars behind.
Loving thoughts beget loving, a cycle pure
and bright,
While unloving thoughts create, a darkness -
such a fright!

So choose the path of kindness, the way of
gentle grace,
And let your heart's true purpose, illuminate
this place.
For in the depths of being, where love and
faith reside,
We find the peace we're seeking, with God as
our only guide.

# Celebration of Love

Within the heart's deep chamber, where faith's
soft whispers dwell,
A truth unfolds, a story that the soul knows
well.

We are one with God, a love that knows no
end,
A radiant, timeless essence, a faithful, trusted
friend.

The world's illusion shatters, when love
becomes our guide,
For fear's dark, grasping tendrils, can no
longer then abide.

Yet egos rise like shadows, with judgments
sharp and cold,
Comparing, labeling...confident in the stories
that it told.

But these are fleeting echoes, not the spirit's
true domain,
We must recall our oneness, and break the
ego's chain.

For in remembering who we are, a light
begins to gleam,
And others find their pathway, within that
sacred dream.

Though terror may surround us, and sorrow
fill the air,
We choose to be compassion, a love beyond
compare.

To lend a helping hand, with kindness in our
gaze,
But not to be consumed, by fear's bewildering
maze.

Acceptance is our anchor, in life's tumultuous
sea,
Let go of what is fleeting, and find serenity.

For what we cannot alter, let gently drift
away,
And trust in God's great wisdom, to guide us
through each day.

Remember, thoughts are seeds, that blossom
in the mind,
Love's gentle whispers nurture, while fear
leaves scars behind.

Loving thoughts beget loving, a cycle pure
and bright,
While unloving thoughts create, only
darkness and fright.

So choose the path of kindness, the way of
gentle grace,
And let your heart's true purpose, illuminate
this place.

For in the depths of being, where love and
faith reside,
We find the peace we're seeking, with God as
our sole guide.